Pet
Parent
Pawffirmations

Pet Parent Pawffirmations

30 promises from you to your beloved dog

Donna Chicone

ANCING PAWS PRESS

Interior photos are credited to the individual pet
parents on the page on which their photo is featured.
The Jazz and Jive tribute photo and the author page
photo are credited to Laurie Erickson.

Library of Congress Control Number: 2017902334
ISBN: 978-0-9968108-3-8

Published by
Dancing Paws Press

Book design by Stacey Aaronson

Printed in the United States of America

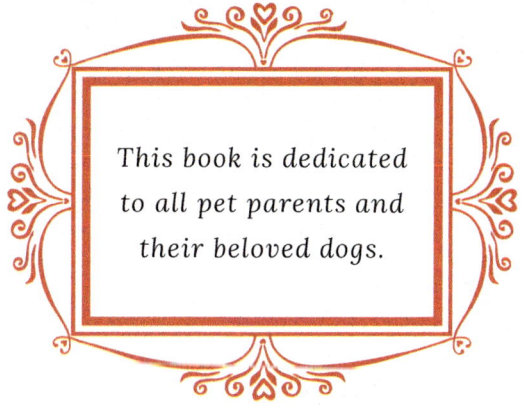

This book is dedicated
to all pet parents and
their beloved dogs.

For Lynn + Mike
+ Cagney + Lacey!
Grateful woofs + Smiles!

Denver Claire

Jazz + Jive

FOR JAZZ & JIVE

♥ ♥ ♥

Being a pet parent brings so much joy to my everyday life. Jazz and Jive, you are both priceless gifts to me, and you are my inspiration to live life to the fullest. To quote Paul Dunn:

> *"My goal in life is to be the person my dog thinks I am."*

You motivate me to live my life with compassion and humility. Your love and loyalty are admirable and so appreciated by me. You inspire me to write about dogs to help make life better for them and their pet parents, and to advocate for the humane treatment of dogs worldwide. I find it incomprehensible how any human being can intentionally neglect or harm such a gentle, sentient being as a dog.

Jazz and Jive, every day I am blessed with the opportunity to look into your eyes and hold you in my arms. Your constant love is healing for me on so many levels. Not only do you make me laugh with your silly antics, but we seem to know what each other is thinking or needs. I don't know how to explain the connection I have with both of you other than to say that I believe other pet parents know exactly what I am referring to. We share a powerful bond and I value this more than you could ever know.

Jazz, I love those moments you walk by me and nudge my leg with your nose as if to say we are partners. Jive, I love those moments you snuggle into my side and look up at me with your sweet eyes. I am so loved by both of you, and I am so grateful and humbled to receive your love. You remind me to live from love and not fear. Loving you makes me a better person, and our shared love is remarkable. Thank you from the depths of my heart. It is with honor that I commit to you every pawffirmation promise in this book.

CONTENTS

♥ ♥ ♥

In Memory
Acknowledgments

$\mathcal{I}$ NTRODUCTION

I simply love dogs. Not only do they greet us with such love and joy when we come home, but they seem to always enjoy being with us. Because that bond and the happiness a dog brings to our life are priceless, I found myself looking for a way to capture that gift to share with pet parents everywhere.

Then one day I had a vision to ask the many pet parents I have contact with send me a picture of their beloved dog – a picture that captured the essence of their relationship together and their dog's personality. To accompany these photos, I envisioned writing promises for specific words that relate to how much our dogs give to us every day, and how we as pet parents can affirm our commitment to our four-legged treasures by reciting these promises. These became the pawffirmations in this book.

This journey has been a delightful one for me. I have been moved to smiles and heartfelt sighs as I gathered the pictures and penned the pawffirmations from my heart. It is my sincere hope that they not only convey a universal commitment from all pet parents to their loving dogs, but will enhance the bond you share with each other.

Joyful Woofs & Smiles!

Donna Chicone

Pet

Parent

Pawffirmations

WELCOME

Briggs

Pet Parents: Bryan & Erin Wagner

pawsitive fact

Responsible breeders, shelters, and rescue groups are the safest resources for finding a dog.

I promise my heart is open to welcoming you into my life. I have researched and planned so your arrival will be joyful and loving. I respect the similarities and the differences between our species. Together we will build a lifelong relationship. I am so happy you are here!

LEARNING

→ *Nicolette* →

Pet Parents: Chrissy & Dallas Tebben

pawsitive fact

Dogs need mental stimulation. Their brains
need to be engaged and challenged just as their
physical bodies do.

I promise to provide you with the
mental stimulation you need. I
will find puzzles, and provide
interactions that will challenge
you to use your brain as well as
your physical abilities. I will
enjoy watching you figure out the
puzzle or how to get the hidden
treat. I will seek out toys and
opportunities that will challenge
your mental abilities. It may even
be pet-assisted therapy work or a
canine sport we will enjoy doing
together.

JOB

Tugboat

5-23-2005 to 10-03-2016

Pet Parents: Sarah & Andy Freeman

pawsitive fact

Dogs need a job. It gives them something
meaningful to look forward to.

I promise to provide you with a job opportunity. We might explore and find a canine activity or perhaps a sport we can enjoy together. You may be a dog who can do pet-assisted therapy work. I will teach you jobs around the house, like bringing your toys in from outside. Whatever it is you are interested in doing, we will do it together and enjoy learning more about each other in the process. Both our worlds will become bigger.

RESPONSIBILITY

→ ····· *Cody* ····· →

Pet Parents: Ann & Brian Aubitz

pawsitive fact

A dog is a huge, lifelong responsibility.

I promise to keep you protected from extreme heat and cold. Whether on leash or in the house, I will know where you are at all times. I will make sure you're supervised when playing with other dogs, and especially with children. I will ensure all your needs are met, including medical care, nutrition, and exercise. I will respect all public areas by picking up behind you, will never leave you alone in a car no matter how long I'll be gone, and will ensure you travel in the safest way possible.

SOCIALIZATION

→ ····· *Cagney & Lacey* ····· →

Pet Parents: Lynn Nelson & Mike Keeler

pawsitive fact

Dogs will have new experiences during their entire lifetime and need our help to learn how to deal with them successfully.

I promise to expose you to new people, places, sounds, shapes, colors, and other dogs so that you can be comfortable greeting new experiences. Socialization will help you to be a calm, happy dog. I also realize socializing you to new experiences will be lifelong. We will do this together!

NUTRITION

→ ····· *Jonesy* ····· →

Pet Parents: John and Pam Solstad

pawsitive fact

Despite any conflicting theories that exist,
it is clear that dogs need two things:
a well-balanced diet and variety.

I promise to find the best food for you. I will read labels and will take time to review the resources that can help me find human-grade quality food, like fresh fruits, vegetables, and protein. I love you and want you by my side for as long as possible. I know a proper diet will contribute to a healthy life for you, my beloved dog, and we will share a long and loving relationship together.

BOND

Cooper

Pet Parents: Bryan & Erin Wagner

pawsitive fact

A bond is developed over time and is
considered interchangeable with the love
we feel for our dogs.

I promise our bond will flourish on a foundation built on trust and mutual respect. I will have positive interactions with you by spending time together, looking into your eyes, and always using loving physical touch and positive training techniques. We will acknowledge each other and relish our time together. I will cherish those times you nudge me with your nose when you walk by me, letting me know we are partners sharing a bond.

RELATIONSHIP

Allie

Pet Parents: John & Angie Orth

pawsitive fact

All relationships take time to grow.
A canine-human relationship is a very special
type between two different species, built on
love and respect.

I promise to be engaged and loyal to you. I will get to know you so well that I will know your favorite spot to be petted and scratched, your favorite treat, and what makes you smile to mention only a few things we will share in our relationship together. We will come to know each other so well we will anticipate each other's needs. I am committed to our relationship to the very end. I will not leave you because you are old or sick. Our relationship is a gift I am ever grateful for.

HOUSE-TRAINING

Honey

Pet Parents: Kathi & Charlie Holmes

pawsitive fact

One of the first behaviors a dog needs to learn
is the acceptable place to go to the bathroom,
which is usually outdoors.

I promise to help you learn what
is expected of you to live
comfortably in this human world.
I will use positive training
techniques to teach you how to tell
me you have to go outside to
eliminate, and I will praise you
for being successful. I will never
punish or demean you if you have
an accident. I love you and
always want you to succeed.

PARENT

Cody

Pet Parent: Nancy Herbst

pawsitive fact

Dogs need a parent, not an alpha pack leader.

I promise to always be your human parent and will never try to dominate you. I know the alpha theory is a myth. I respect you and the fact that you depend on me to feed, shelter, and love you. I will never abuse that dependency, and I will always be there when you need me as your loving, respectful, human pet parent.

EXERCISE

Erik, Rim & Simmer
Pet Parent: Laurie Erickson

pawsitive fact

Dogs need physical exercise to build muscle tone and maintain overall health. Exercise is mutually beneficial for dogs and pet parents.

I promise to exercise with you. We will go for daily walks together, and I will provide you a fenced-in backyard to run in or take you to a park where you can run freely and safely. I will make sure you have opportunities to play with other dogs by scheduling play dates with our canine friends. Obesity is the number one health concern for dogs and humans, so together we will get the physical exercise we need to maintain our proper weight and good health.

PERSONALITY

Henry

Pet Parents: Nick & Nikki Aune

pawsitive fact

Every dog has a unique personality,
and no two dogs are alike.

I promise to respect and enjoy your personality. Learning what you like and don't like will be a fun journey we will take together. Whether you are shy or outgoing, curious or mellow, we will come to enjoy each other. You will make me laugh with your sense of humor and funny antics, and I will value your distinct, one-of-a-kind personality.

DIFFERENCES

Grizz

Pet Parent: Dianne Dahl

pawsitive fact

Canine and Human are two different species.
Understanding and respecting the differences
makes enjoying the similarities more fun.

I promise not to treat you like a human child when you are clearly being a dog. I will focus on you as a dog and learn what makes you different from humans, like your distinct anatomy and ways of communicating. I will enjoy the canine-human similarities, such as your sentient ability to feel love, fear, pain, and other emotions. I am grateful for the loving diversity you bring into my life.

COMMUNICATION

→ ······ *Tug Boat* ······ →

Pet Parents: Cole & Bryan Williams

pawsitive fact

Dogs have their language and humans have
theirs. Learning to communicate human to dog
is definitely possible and highly enjoyable.
Basic obedience training is essential to
good communication.

I promise to learn everything I can about communicating with dogs. I will learn what your body language signs mean, and I will look into your eyes and speak to you, teaching you behavioral associations with my words. You can learn sit, stay, off, come, and many other words and their meanings. The more time we spend together, the more our communication will grow. Developing communication will be so much fun for both of us.

TOUCH

Simmer

Pet Parent: Laurie Erickson

pawsitive fact

Touch is to be loving and respectful at all times
with our dogs. Humane treatment involves
positive training techniques and loving touch,
which is the opposite of physical abuse.

I promise I will never abuse you physically. I communicate love and respect through my hands and will never use a physical object to hit you. Holding and petting you will allow me to get to know your body and if there is anything abnormal that may need medical attention. Touch is essential to love, and loving you and petting you will bring joy to both of us.

LOVE

Curry

Pet Parent: Kate An Hunter

pawsitive fact

Dogs are known for their unconditional love for their people. The joy of love shared between a dog and their pet parent is priceless.

I promise to love you and protect you always. You give your love so freely, and I will always treasure and respect this gift. My love for you will be unwavering, and I will show it by always meeting your needs and keeping you safe when you need me to. I am grateful for your unconditional love and give in return my forever love to you.

BELONGINGS

Tendo

Pet Parents: Laura & Christina Sterling

pawsitive fact

Dogs' belongings are a statement that he/she is a true member of a family.

I promise you will have your own place to sleep, a box full of play toys and chew toys, a food table to eat from, a yard to run in or a safe place to run and play away from home, and your own toothbrush and grooming area. You are a loved member of our family and will have your own belongings, just as other family members have theirs.

RESPECT

→ ····· **Lola & Oscar** ····· ←

Pet Parents: Jeff Lugerner & Karen Cooley

pawsitive fact

Mutual respect is essential for a successful
relationship between a pet parent and a dog.

❧ ♥ ♥ ♥ ❧

I promise to respect you for the
sentient being you are. I respect
that you feel love, fear, pain, joy,
and many other feelings. I respect
the differences between our species
and I respect our similarities.
You are a very special being in
my life. I am humbled and
grateful to be your partner on this
life journey together.

❧ ♥ ♥ ♥ ❧

NURTURING

→ ···· *Maddie Mae* ···· →

Pet Parents: Karl & Pat Wall

pawsitive fact

Dogs respond significantly to positive verbal
praise and petting, as well as to treats.

I promise to nurture you with
positive touch and words using a
loving and encouraging tone in my
voice. What I say and do will
express the love I feel for you
always. I will help you develop
into a confident and happy dog.
Your physical and emotional
safety will be a primary
concern at all times.
You fill my life with joy!

TRAINING

→ ····· *Manny & Bella* ····· →

Pet Parent: Sarah Falk

pawsitive fact

Basic obedience training is a dog's right
and a pet parent's responsibility.

I promise to use positive training techniques always. I want you to have good canine manners, so I will lovingly teach you to sit, stay, come, leave it, and other behaviors that will help you feel comfortable and know what is expected of you. I will make sure you learn basic obedience skills that create a foundation of behavior you can build on to learn even more. I know training is a lifelong commitment. You deserve this training and I will make sure you receive it with love.

MONEY

Matthew

Pet Parent: Judy Super

pawsitive fact

Having a dog costs money. Food, vet fees,
training, equipment (leashes, collars, etc.) are
crucial to consider before you bring a
dog into your life.

I promise I will research the costs involved in having a dog like you in my life. Large dogs eat more and have higher veterinarian costs, and different breeds have certain health issues. I will learn everything I can about caring for you, and I will make sure I have money set aside to pay for those emergency situations that can arise. I will adjust my budget to accommodate your needs. I don't want to lose you because I cannot afford to care for you.

HOPE

Lacey

Pet Parents: Ruth & David Levy

pawsitive fact

Hope springs eternal when you look into the
eyes of a dog. Dogs who have been abused and
neglected seem able to forgive and move on. It
is as if they never lose hope about finding a
home where they will be loved.

I promise to share your hope for our relationship, and I will give you every reason to feel positive about us. We will make loving memories together and will enjoy growing old together. Hope will be a central part of our relationship and time together.

PLAY

Kaya

Pet Parents: Kris & Paul Muyskens

pawsitive fact

Playtime is fundamental to a positive quality of life for dogs.

I promise to play with you and make sure you have play opportunities with other dogs. You will have your own toy box with your very own soft toys and chew toys. I will take time to play tug, fetch, find-it, or whatever favorite games you enjoy. We will develop our favorite playtimes and enjoy seeing each other smile and have fun together.

LISTENING

Lucy & Ricky

Pet Parent: Jean Knox

pawsitive fact

Dogs have keen hearing. They watch our body
language to learn what we are saying, in
addition to hearing our human words.

I promise to speak to you in a calm tone. Raising my voice is not necessary for you to hear me, as your hearing is very sensitive. I will also work to learn your body language so that I understand what you are trying to express. We will both learn to listen to what each other is saying to find a common language.

TRUST

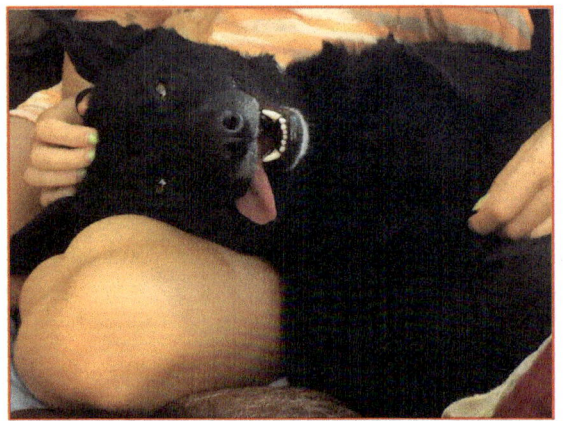

Leilani

Pet Parent: Evey Krammer-Carlson

pawsitive fact

Trust is a significant bond built and respected
between a dog and a pet parent.

I promise to build a bond of trust between us. I will trust you and give you every reason to trust me. I will learn to have faith in your ability to make good decisions for yourself, and I will also know when you need me to help you. Trust works both ways and I am committed to build and respect our mutual bond. I will never abuse you physically or emotionally. I will only give you reason to trust me and not fear me.

GROOMING

Tank

Pet Parents: Ken & Debra Hertz

pawsitive fact

A clean dog is a healthy and happy dog.
Regular grooming can reduce shedding and
promote healthier skin and coat.

I promise to keep you groomed, not only for health reasons but also because I want you to look and feel good about yourself. If you have hair, it will matt and smell if you are not bathed regularly. If you shed, frequent grooming will help reduce your shedding. Spending time touching your body through brushing will help me know if there are any changes to your anatomy I should be concerned about. If I cannot groom you, I will take you to a groomer you like.

HEALTH

→ ······ *Satine* ······ →

Pet Parents: Kally & Ryan Muenster

pawsitive fact

Dogs need a yearly health exam just as
humans do. Health checks and disease
prevention is vital for dogs.

I promise to take you to our veterinarian for your annual exam every year. I will get you the medical help you need anytime you are sick or injured. I will learn everything I can about your breed/breeds' influence and how that can impact your health. I will research vitamins and supplements and only give you what you need to be healthy and strong. I will learn to brush your teeth and brush them regularly. I want you to be healthy so you can enjoy your life.

TIME

Ricki

Pet Parent: Judy Super

pawsitive fact

All relationships require time together.
A relationship with a dog requires time together
to build trust and a loving bond.

I promise to spend quality time with you every day. You are my partner and I am committed to developing our relationship. I know I am your focus and that you want more than anything else to spend time with me. I will honor and respect that desire by making sure my schedule and life activities allow us time together every day. As a puppy you will need a lot of my time to take care of you and teach you many "firsts." Our time together will be a joy for both of us.

CELEBRATION

Fiona

Pet Parent: Sue Hardman

pawsitive fact

Celebrating life makes one feel valued and even
special. This applies to our dogs as well.

I promise I will always celebrate the day you came into the world, or the approximate date if I'm unsure. I will make your birthday meaningful by making you a special food or getting you a doggie cake, having a party, and giving you gifts. I will celebrate every day with you as we live out our life journey together. Life with a dog is the best life, and life with you is amazing!

GOOD-BYE

Beauregard

Pet Parent: Sharon Middendorf

pawsitive fact

When our dogs are ready to leave is the time they need us the most. Saying good-bye is the hardest part of loving.

I promise I will help you say good-bye with dignity. I will not let you live in pain and poor quality of life because I have difficulty letting you go. I will be strong and be there for you when it is your time to leave. I will let my face be the last face you see and my touch be the last touch you feel. Your paw prints will forever be on my heart.

In memory

This book is in memory of Amy Allwine, a friend and trainer who loved dogs and their pet parents. Among her many contributions, Amy brought the sport of Canine Nose Work to the state of Minnesota, which so many of us are very grateful for. Amy left us much too soon, but in her time here, she made a significant positive impact on every life she touched, both canine and human. Amy, you are loved and missed.

$\mathcal{A}$CKNOWLEDGMENTS

First, I want to acknowledge my editor and book designer Stacey Aaronson. Neither my first book nor this one would be possible without her. Stacey approaches every project she works on with a personal commitment to make it the best product it could ever be. Her tech savvy and her creative and intuitive talents make the journey so exciting, and I completely trust her with helping me birth my "baby." When I realized I would be writing this second book, I knew without a doubt Stacey would be my partner; in fact, I couldn't wait to begin working with her. I may have to write more books to keep repeating what is always a creative, joyful experience. Thank you, Stacey, for your strong work ethic, kind heart, and obvious talent, and for helping bring my dream to life. I am most grateful.

My family has been a constant support to all my endeavors and me. My husband Jim, my son Brandon, my like-a-daughter Becky, and my grandsons Dominic and Leo, thank you for your love and belief in me. It is wonderful to know you are always there to give me feedback and cheer me on. Our family is our unbreakable connection to each other and I am blessed and grateful for this.

I wish to thank all the pet parents who have sent me pictures of their fantastic dogs. I also want to thank them for being such great pet parents – for giving their dog(s) abundant love and making sure all their needs are met. I could sense the pride you feel for your dogs through the pictures you sent me. Your eagerness to share your relationship is a gift not only for me, but also for all the people who read this book. You are role models for other pet parents and for those who aspire to be. Thank you for being that special person in your dog's life.

My deepest gratitude goes to:

Ann and Brian Aubitz &
Cody

Nick & Nikki Aune &
Henry

Jeff Lugerner and Karen Cooley &
Lola & Oscar

Dianne Dahl &
Grizz

Laurie Erickson &
Erik, Rim & Simmer

Sarah Falk &
Manny & Bella

Sarah and Andy Freeman &
Tugboat

Sue Hardman &
Fiona

Nancy Herbst &
Cody

Ken and Debra Hertz &
Tank

Kathi and Charlie Holmes &
Honey

Kate An Hunter &
Curry

Jean Knox &
Lucy & Ricky

Evey Krammer-Carlson &
Leilani

Ruth and David Levy &
Lacey

Sharon Middendorf &
Beauregard

Kally and Ryan Muenster &
Satine

Kris and Paul Muyskens &
Kaya

Lynn Nelson and Mike Keeler &
Cagney & Lacey

John and Angie Orth &
Allie

John and Pam Solstad &
Jonesy

Laura and Christina Sterling &
Tendo

Judy Super &
Matthew & Ricki

Chrissy and Dallas Tebben &
Nicolette

Bryan and Erin Wagner &
Briggs & Cooper

Karl and Pat Wall &
Maddie Mae

Cole and Bryan Williams &
Tug Boat

About the Author

Donna Chicone is the award-winning author of *Being a Super Pet Parent*. She is an animal advocate, entertainer, TedX speaker, and pet parent — a joy and responsibility she takes very seriously.

After leaving a twenty-three-year career in corporate America, Donna began her quest to help make life better for dogs and the humans who love them. This led to the creation and hosting of the TV show, *The Dog Show with Jazz*, which ran for forty-eight episodes with her then sole Portuguese water dog as co-host. During the last year of the show, her second Portuguese water dog, Jive, joined them.

Committed to ensuring Jazz and Jive have a purpose, both are trained as Animal Assisted Therapy dogs and currently work with children aged two and a half to five in a trauma pre-school setting, as well as in a facility for adults with developmental disabilities. To keep them mentally and physically challenged, both dogs also attend ongoing Canine Nose Work classes and compete in the sport as well.

Donna's advocacy for all animals is expressed in her lifestyle of eating a vegetarian diet and supporting efforts to end cruelty to farm and wild animals. Her passion for the welfare of dogs, as well as her desire to educate others that all animals are sentient beings who feel pain, fear, joy, and love, motivated her to write *Being a Super Pet Parent*, which won the 2016 National Indie Excellence Award. Her sincere wish is for every dog to be loved by a human who understands and embraces the commitment of having a dog in his or her life. When humans make this relatable connection with animals, they achieve a mutual respect for each other, whereby cruelty to animals has less opportunity to exist.

Donna lives with her husband in Minnesota where they enjoy spending time with their one son, his wife, and two grandsons.

jazzandjive.com

CPSIA information can be obtained
at www.ICGtesting.com
Printed in the USA
LVOW01s0807020417
529239LV00007B/7/P